THE TAO OF MEOW

THE TAO OF MEOW

LIFE'S LITTLE INSTRUCTION
BOOK FUR CATS

WRITTEN BY MARGARET GEE   ILLUSTRATED BY JON HAWLEY

TEN SPEED PRESS / BERKELEY, CALIFORNIA

TEN SPEED PRESS
P. O. Box 7123
Berkeley, California 94707

Cover and text design by Margaret Gee and Jon Hawley

Library of Congress Cataloging-in-Publication Data

Gee, Margaret.
The Tao of Meow / Margaret Gee and Jon Hawley.
p. cm.
ISBN 0-89815-588-6
1. Cats—Humor. 2. Conduct of life—humor. 3. Cats—Caricatures and cartoons.
4. Australian wit and humor, Pictorial. I. Hawley, Jon. II. Title.
PN6231.C23G44 1993
818'.5402—dc20
93-21197
CIP

Printed in Singapore

1 2 3 4 5 — 97 96 95 94 93

Dedi**CAT**ion

For
Kit Kat and Sardine
and in loving memory of
Bibi.

Margaret Gee

WAKE UP WITH THE BIRDS.

AROUSE YOUR MISTRESS GENTLY.

ASK AND YOU WILL RECEIVE.

ENJOY EVERY MORSEL.

CLEANSE YOURSELF.

BREATHE EASY.

SLEEP

AROUND.

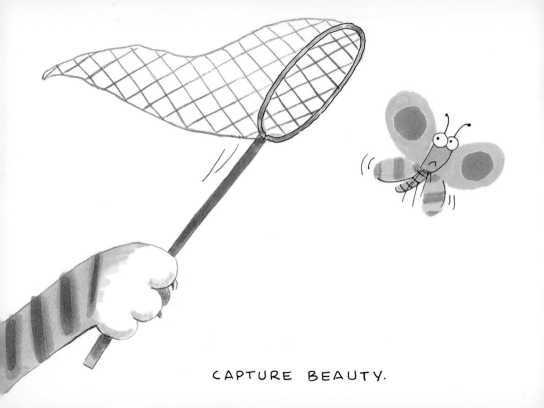

CAPTURE BEAUTY.

CLAW YOUR WAY TO THE TOP.

MASTER A NEW LANGUAGE.

VIBRATE WITH JOY.

WEAR A HAT IN SUMMER.

IMMERSE YOURSELF IN KNOWLEDGE.

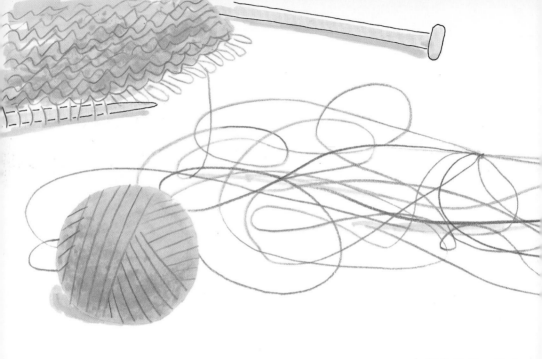

LEARN TO

PULL STRINGS.

KNOW THAT ANIMAL RIGHTS STOP WITH FLEAS.

SAVE WATER — RARELY BATHE.

CELEBRATE YOUR BIRTHDAYS.

BE LOVING.

NEVER UNDERESTIMATE THE

IMPORTANCE OF PAW PLAY.

TRIM YOUR NAILS.

LEARN TO SWIM.

WATCH THE GRASS GROW.

DON'T PANIC.

THINK

POSITIVE.

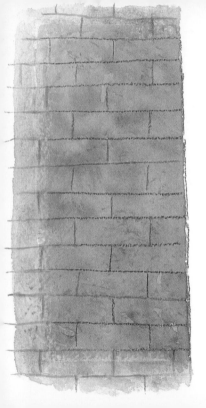

LOOK BEFORE

YOU LEAP.

BE HOSPITABLE.

KNOW YOUR DARK SIDE.

DRINK IN MODERATION.

DON'T MOVE IN THE WRONG CIRCLES.

SAY NO TO DRUGS.

CHANNEL YOUR ENERGIES.

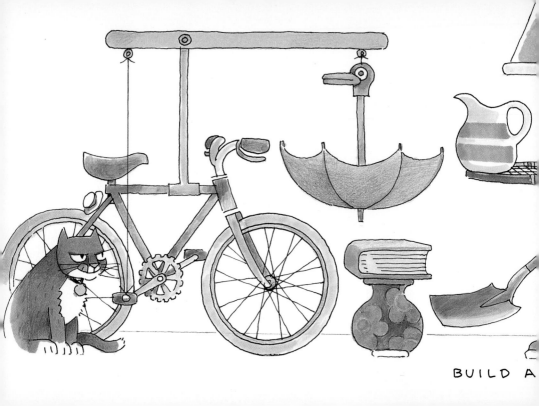

BUILD A

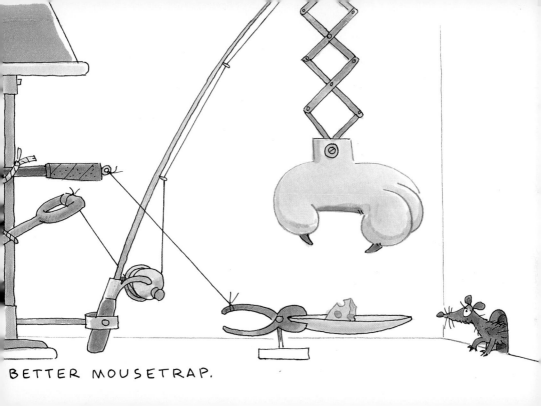

BETTER MOUSETRAP.

FANTASIZE.

HELP OPEN THE CHRISTMAS PRESENTS.

BEWARE OF GLUTTONY.

DON'T BITE OFF MORE THAN YOU CAN CHEW.

KNOW YOUR ENEMY.

DON'T RAT ON YOUR FRIENDS.

FERTILIZE THE GARDEN REGULARLY.

WHEN THEY'RE OUT, USE THEIR LITTER BOX.

DARE TO

BE DIFFERENT.

LEARN A MUSICAL INSTRUMENT.

LEVITATE.

TRANSCEND TECHNOLOGY.

COMMUNICATE

ATTRACT OPPOSITES.

ENCOURAGE CODEPENDENCY.

MERCIFUL.

HAVE A MIND LIKE A STEEL TRAP.

DON'T RUB PEOPLE THE WRONG WAY.

PAMPURR YOURSELF

FOR THE BODY IS THE TEMPLE OF THE SOUL.

FEED THE

BIRDS.

ALWAYS DRESS FOR DINNER.

AVOID EXERCISING ON A FULL STOMACH.

KILL TIME CREATIVELY.

WET
CEMENT

LEAVE YOUR MARK.

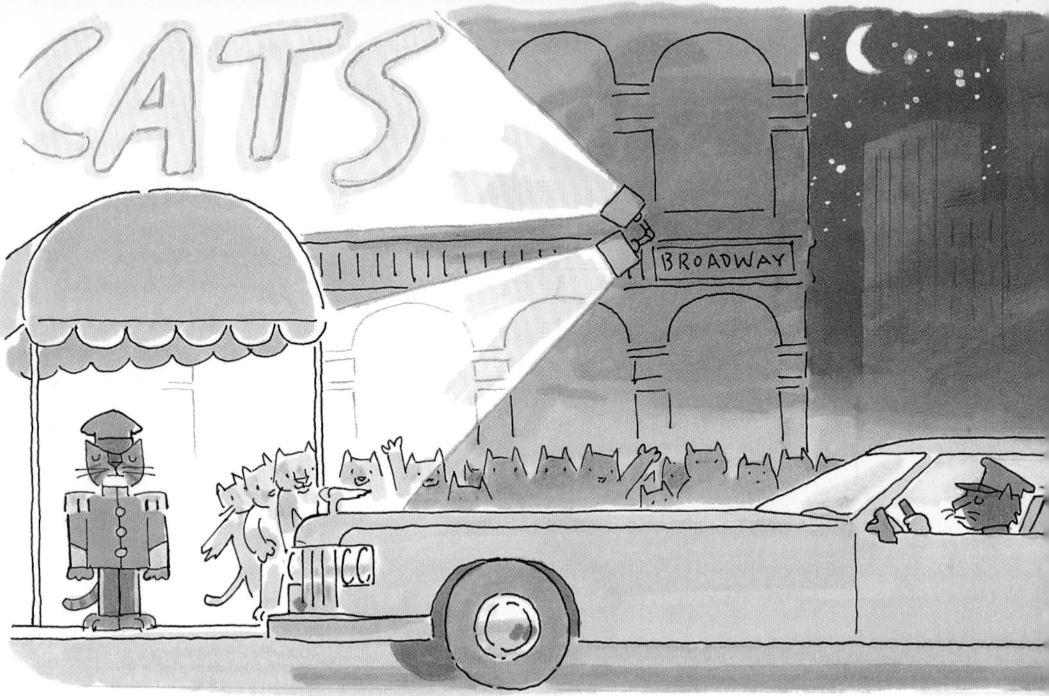
CATS
BROADWAY
CC

STOP THE SHOW.

LOVE YOUR KITTENS.

SLEEP UNDER THE STARS.

JOIN A

CHOIR.

DANCE BY THE LIGHT OF THE MOON.

HELP OUT AT HOME.

FOLLOW YOUR OWN PATH.